Art Director: Rita Marshall
Book Design: Stephanie Blumenthal
Text Adapted and Edited from the French language by Kitty Benedict
Library of Congress Cataloging-in-Publication Data
Benedict, Kitty.
Wolf/written by Andrienne Soutter-Perrot; adapted for the American reader
by Kitty Benedict; illustrated by François Crozat.
Summary: Describes the physical characteristics, life cycle, and behavior
of the wolf.
ISBN 1-56846-042-2
1. Wolves—Juvenile literature. [1. Wolves.]
I. Soutter-Perrot, Andrienne. II. Crozat, François, ill. III. Title.
QC737.C22B45   1992
599.74'442--dc20   92-5979

WLF

WRITTEN BY

ANDRIENNE SOUTTER-PERROT

ILLUSTRATED BY

FRANÇOIS CROZAT

CREATIVE EDITIONS

All animals must eat in order to live. Animals that eat plants are called herbivores. Animals that eat other animals are called carnivores.

A carnivore's mouth is full of sharp teeth that cut, tear, and grind flesh and bones. The pointed fangs in front are called canine teeth. The strong ones in back are called flesh teeth.

The very first animal to live with humans was a carnivore—the dog.

Carnivores may have the same kind of teeth, but not all carnivores are alike. For example, a cat is very different from a dog in the way that it looks, moves, and acts.

Carnivores in the cat family, like lions or panthers, are called felines, while members of the dog family are called canines.

Coyotes, jackals, foxes, and wolves are all canines.

WHAT DOES A WOLF LOOK LIKE?

A full-grown wolf is the size of a large dog. Long-legged and deep-chested, it can run for hours at a steady and tireless pace.

Wolf fur changes color and texture as a wolf ages. Wolf pups are born dark, then turn gray and tan. Adults have mixed coats of black, white, and yellow. Older wolves turn silver.

When a wolf is upset, its mane bristles, its ears prick up, its tail points, and its yellow eyes gleam intensely.

A wolf does not bark like a dog or a fox. It howls instead. A wolf's howl may sound like a mournful song.

HOW DO WOLVES GROW UP?

During the winter, wolves live in a group called a pack. This makes it easier to hunt big game like deer or wild boar.

In early spring, the male wolf in charge of the pack chooses a female as his mate. The younger wolves may drift off in different directions.

The male and female travel great distances in search of a den. They look for a sheltered but sunny spot, near a source of water.

The she-wolf digs a shallow hole, then lines it with grass, ferns, moss, and hair from her stomach. Two months after mating, she gives birth to several young.

Wolf pups are born blind and deaf. At first, all they do is nurse and sleep. After about two weeks their eyes open and they begin to walk around.

The mother wolf tends her pups carefully. She rarely leaves them alone, even to get a drink.

The male wolf brings food to his mate. Then he lies down in front of the den, his eyes half closed. He is guarding the den.

When the pups are a little bigger, they run everywhere. The mother wolf carries them back to the den in her mouth, or nudges them along with her paws.

If the mother wolf senses that her pups are in danger, she acts quickly, lifting each one by the scruff of the neck and moving it to a safe hiding place.

Wolf pups are very playful and affectionate, chasing, nipping, and climbing on their patient parents.

When the pups are two months old, they stop nursing and learn to eat meat. At first the parents chew, swallow, and spit up meat for the pups to eat.

Soon the parents bring whole pieces of meat. The pups rush and tear at the food, growling all the while. Later, they learn to hunt and kill on their own.

By the end of autumn, the wolf pups can manage on their own, but they still spend the winter with their parents. They are joined by the young wolves from the previous winter.

HOW DO WOLVES LIVE?

The size of a wolf pack's hunting territory is determined by how much game is around and how big the pack is.

In the winter, wolves do not eat often, but they are able to eat a great deal when they find game. Weak or sick animals are the first ones they kill.

Wolves attack each other only if they are defending their pups or their territory. When two wolves fight, the battle is over as soon as the loser exposes his throat to the winner.

Once there were many wolves all over the world. Today there are only a few left.

Nature needs wolves in order to stay healthy and balanced.